WRITING IN SCIENCE

 GLOBE FEARON EDUCATIONAL PUBLISHER
A Division of Simon & Schuster
Upper Saddle River, New Jersey

Executive Editor: Barbara Levadi

Project Editors: Lynn W. Kloss, Laura Baselice, and Bernice Golden

Writer: Sandra Widener

Production Manager: Penny Gibson

Production Editor: Nicole Cypher

Marketing Managers: Sandra Hutchison and Nancy Surridge

Interior Electronic Design: Richard Puder Design

Illustrators: Accurate Art and Andre V. Malok

Electronic Page Production: Paradigm Design

Cover Design: Mimi Raihl

Acknowledgments
p. 16 (top): courtesy of Gillian Aldrich; (bottom): courtesy of
Reuters/Bettmann; **p. 60** (top): courtesy of Swiss National Tourist
Office; (bottom): courtesy of F. B. Grunzweig, Photo Researchers;
p. 68: courtesy of UPI/ Bettmann.

Printed in the United States of America.
    4 5 6 7 8 9 10 99 98
BF2

ISBN: 0835-91901-3

 GLOBE FEARON EDUCATIONAL PUBLISHER
A Division of Simon & Schuster
Upper Saddle River, New Jersey

Contents

Science in Everyday Life

Applying Science

Science at Work

To the Student

Scientists write every day. They write the results of their research. They explain science to others. Scientists communicate so that what they know can help people improve their lives. They write in many areas, ranging from finding cures for disease to making better spaceships. Even if you don't become a scientist, you may be writing about science. You may have to write a letter to someone explaining how a machine works or write a report about the weather for a boss.

The lessons in this book will give you a chance to practice writing about science. (See the Writing Checklist on page 75 for general help with writing.) You'll learn skills for school, such as how to take science notes and how to answer science essay questions. You'll also learn science writing skills that you'll need throughout your life, from explaining a chart to writing persuasive letters.

Writing in Science is divided into six units that cover science writing and science skills. There are also lessons to help you improve your everyday science writing.

Writing Skills for Science. In this unit, you'll practice taking notes so that you can remember the important information you learn from books and from speakers. You'll also learn to explain science through summarizing science articles and taking notes about your observations.

Developing Science Skills. This unit will show you how to make an inference and then write about it. You'll also create and explain a bar graph. Finally, four of the lessons in this unit walk you through the process of thinking out a science experiment and writing what you learn.

Writing a Science Report. Writing a report is a great way to think about and understand a science topic. The lessons in this unit break down the steps a writer goes through to create a report. By the time you finish, you will know how to choose a topic, research it, write it, and revise it to create a polished paper.

Science in Everyday Life. This unit will show you how you use science daily. For example, you might test cleaning products to see which one works best. You might also use science to tell if claims for an ad are truthful or to advise a camp cook which snacks are healthful.

Applying Science. You apply your knowledge of science to explain scientific principles and gather and analyze data. You'll also see how the forces of the Earth affect the landscape and use your knowledge of science to write a press release.

Science at Work. Almost every job uses science in some way. For example, in this unit you'll write a persuasive flyer, interpret a table as a vet's assistant, and write a science book for children.

Writing about science can help you understand the world. It is also something you'll use in your daily life. With practice, you can become a better writer. We hope that this book will help you learn this process.

LESSON 1
Keeping a Journal
Nature Notes

What You'll LEARN

Keeping a journal is one way scientists remember their thoughts, record their observations, and interpret what they see.

What You'll DO

You'll need a Science Journal, which can be part of your notebook. Start a section called "Nature Notes." Then use this checklist to help you choose a place to observe. When you observe, you notice details.

> Is this a place I can observe whenever I want?
> Is there a wide variety of plant and animal life there?
> Have I chosen a place small enough to observe carefully?

Visit your place for six weeks. By observing the changes that happen to one small area of the Earth and writing what you see over several weeks, you will be doing several important tasks. You will be using your senses to observe. You will also be recording your data. Finally, you will be making interpretations about what you see. An interpretation is an explanation of what you observe.

Your observations will be more valuable if you use precise words, describe what you see accurately, and notice details such as size, shape, and color.

Here is one example of a student's nature notes:

May 13: This week I noticed three new plants. Ants, earthworms, and ladybugs were crawling in the dirt. I also saw a bee on a dandelion that bloomed this week. The dandelion was the first one to bloom. The bloom must have attracted the bee. The soil is wet from all the rain, and the plants look greener than they have. I think the conditions are good for plants now. The weather is warmer, there is more sun every day, and the plants seem to like all the rain. Maybe if there were a fence up, it would stop the joggers from killing the plants.

Crocus

Daffodils

Secund

What You'll WRITE Ask yourself these questions. Answer them on these pages the first time. Then answer the same questions in your journal every time you visit your place. That way, you will be able to compare your observations over time.

1. What plants do you see? What is their condition? (You may want to make a drawing of the plants and identify them later.) _____

_____

_____

_____

2. What animals do you observe? What are they doing? _____

_____

_____

_____

3. What is the weather like? How is the weather affecting the plants and animals?

_____

_____

_____

_____

Add your own observations and comments to your journal notes. As you keep track of your area, add these questions to your list. They will help you interpret what you see.

4. How is the area changing? Why is it changing? _____

_____

_____

_____

5. What signs of a change in season are there? _____

_____

_____

6. Does this area need protection from people? Why or why not? _____

_____

_____

_____

After you have taken notes for six weeks, see Keeping a Journal: Nature Notes II, in Lesson 7, on page 14.

LESSON 2 Using a Diagram Organizing Ideas

What You'll LEARN Placing ideas into a diagram, or graphic organizer, can help you understand the key points and supporting information, or details, in a scientific article.

What You'll DO Diagrams can show the connections among ideas. Here is one diagram that shows the main ideas and supporting evidence from an article about hazardous waste. Study the way this diagram is constructed.

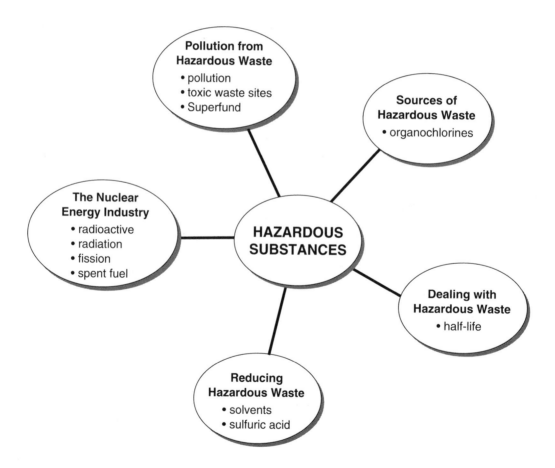

Notice that the subject, hazardous substances, is in the center circle. The article's main ideas are in circles attached to the center circle. Under each main idea supporting evidence, or details, are listed.

What You'll WRITE Make a graphic organizer, and then use it to explain the main points and details in an article or chapter.

1. Draw a circle for the main topic of the article. Draw a circle for each main point of the article. Under each main idea, list the details that support each. After you have finished your diagram, check your work against this list:

   ☐ Is the subject of the article or chapter in the center of the diagram?

   ☐ Are the main points in circles attached to the subject circle?

   ☐ Are supporting points or evidence listed under each main point?

2. After you have finished your organizer, use it to write a sentence or two that explains each main point and the details in the article or chapter. _____

_____

_____

_____

_____

_____

LESSON 3 Taking Notes: Reading

What You'll LEARN

Taking notes from something you read isn't a skill you'll use only in school. Often, people take notes from material they're reading to help them in their jobs. For example, someone might have to take notes from a magazine article to report to her boss about what's new in an industry.

What You'll DO

Use a chapter of a science book that you are using in your classroom to try out this way of taking notes.

What You'll WRITE

Before you begin to take notes, skim what you're reading to find out the general outline. To skim a piece of writing, look at the titles and subtitles. Then look at the pictures and graphs. Go back to the beginning and read the introduction. Then read the final paragraphs, which often summarize the information. Write your notes here.

1. What is the main topic of the article or chapter?_____

_____

_____

_____

_____

As you take notes, keep these tips in mind:

Don't write in sentences.

Write important words or phrases.

Write down main points.

Write down the details that support each point.

2. What are details or supporting evidence in the chapter?_____

_____

_____

_____

_____

3. Select another chapter from the science book. Skim for main ideas and details. When you have finished, you should have a good idea of what is important in the reading you have just done. Write notes here.

Major point: _____

_____

Details or supporting evidence: _____

_____

_____

Major point: _____

_____

Details or supporting evidence: _____

_____

_____

Main point: _____

_____

Details or supporting evidence: _____

_____

_____

If the chapter or article has more than three main points, use another piece of paper to complete your notes.

4. Go back over your notes. You might want to underline the most important words in what you wrote. Then use your notes to write a summary paragraph that explains what you learned in your reading. _____

_____

_____

_____

_____

_____

_____

_____

_____

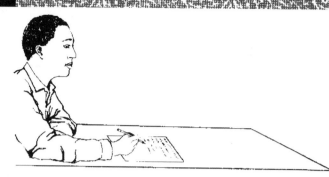

LESSON 4 Taking Notes Listening

What You'll LEARN

Taking notes while you listen is a skill you will use throughout your life. At some point, you will probably have to write what a car mechanic tells you or listen to directions that explain how to go from one place to another. This activity will show you how to take good notes while you're listening to someone.

What You'll DO

You might choose to fill in this outline while you are listening to someone talk about science. You could also fill in these pages while listening to a television show about a scientific topic.

What You'll WRITE

Before you begin, answer this list of questions to help you think about what you will be hearing.

1. What is the topic?_____

_____

2. What do I already know about the topic?_____

_____

_____

_____

_____

3. What is the speaker's purpose or the purpose of the show?_____

_____

_____

_____

4. What audience does the speaker intend to reach?_____

_____

_____

_____

5. What information do I hope to gain?_____

_____

_____

_____

As you listen to the speaker or show, keep the following questions in mind. Fill in the answers as you hear them.

6. What are the key points the speaker is making? (You can tell when a speaker is making an important point when he or she uses phrases like "There are three reasons . . .")

_____

_____

_____

_____

_____

_____

_____

7. What details does the speaker give for each key point? Write evidence for each point the speaker makes. _____

_____

_____

_____

_____

_____

_____

8. At the end of a presentation, a speaker usually will restate important information. How does the speaker summarize his or her speech?_____

_____

_____

_____

_____

_____

_____

LESSON 5 Understanding Science
Summarizing an Article

What You'll LEARN Being able to understand an article about science and summarize it comes in handy. For example, you may read an article about sunscreen and want to give your friend a summary of what you've read.

What You'll DO Read the excerpts below. Then write a summary of what each says. A *summary* is a brief statement of the important ideas in a piece of writing. When you summarize, look for the key ideas, and use as few words as possible to state them. Use your own words.

What You'll WRITE Write a summary for each selection.

Bats Stalk Mexican Livestock
by Nancy Nusser

ALAMOS, Mexico—Every once in a while, someone sees one—a vampire bat flying in the soft night air in search of blood.

But more often in recent months, they've struck unseen, dropping from moonless skies to feed on cows sleeping in the broad, dark fields.

For the first time in more than ten years, rabid vampire bats are stalking livestock in the surrounding hills and plains.

Since last fall, 300 to 340 cows have died from what appears to be rabies transmitted by vampire bats, according to state government estimates. In a place where cattle are people's livelihood, what residents now call "the plague" is serious business.

Cox News Service

---

1. Summary: _____

_____

_____

_____

_____

_____

Sea Level Rising Faster Than Thought

WASHINGTON—A satellite has detected a sea-level rise of more than a tenth of an inch in each of the past two years, about twice that measured by land-based instruments over the last century.

Researchers said yesterday that they are uncertain if this rise is caused by a general warming of the Earth's climate or if it is a short-term effect. But if the trend continues, said one expert, "it could be very, very significant."

A rise in the sea level is one of the major effects from any general warming of the global climate.

The Associated Press

2. Summary: _____

_____

_____

_____

Friends of Whales Fight a Salt Factory
by Paul Sherman

LA LAGUNA, Mexico—Every winter, thousands of gray whales make the long trip from Alaska to breed in a handful of inlets of the Baja California peninsula.

But Mexican officials say one of these inlets would also be perfect for producing salt from seawater. They have proposed construction of the world's largest plant for this purpose along the shore of the San Ignacio Lagoon, one of the whales' most important breeding areas, which is part of a national reserve.

The proposal is at the center of a national debate over whether Mexico should loosen its environmental standards to help salvage [save] its economy.

The New York Times

3. Summary: _____

_____

_____

_____

LESSON 6 Keeping a Journal
Household Science

What You'll LEARN

From using simple machines to watching a bird build a nest, you see science at work every day. By keeping notes about what you see around you, you can understand scientific principles in everyday life.

What You'll DO

During the next few days, use a section of your science journal to record the science you see. First, you'll write what you observe. Then you'll infer, or make a good guess about, what scientific principle is at work.

Here's an entry from one student's journal:

September 8: Today I sat in the kitchen for a few minutes and tried to write down every time I saw a scientific principle at work. Here's what I saw:

1. I saw my brother turn on a light switch. When he did that, he completed an electrical circuit, which meant that the lights went on.

2. I watched my dog eat his dinner and drink from his water dish. A few minutes later, he barked to go out. From that, I could see some principles of life science at work. My dog needed to eat and drink to live. Then he went outside to eliminate wastes his body didn't need.

3. My brother put an ice cube into a soft drink. A few minutes later, the ice cube began to melt. That showed the change from a solid to a liquid state because of a change in temperature.

What You'll WRITE Try to observe in different places as you keep your journal. Ask yourself these questions. Answer them on these pages. Later, you can take notes in your journal.

1. Where do I see a principle of earth science at work? (Examples might include weather conditions.) _____

_____

_____

_____

2. Where do I see a principle of chemistry at work? (Examples might be the use of cleaners, cooking, or rust that shows metal changing.) _____

_____

_____

_____

3. Where do I see a principle of life science at work? (Examples might include the life processes of animals, including humans, and plant reproduction.) _____

_____

_____

_____

4. Where do I see a principle of force and energy at work? (Examples might include simple and compound machines, light and sound, and electricity.) _____

_____

_____

_____

5. What examples do I see of several scientific principles at work at the same time?

_____

_____

_____

6. In what ways have scientists' understanding and discoveries changed the world around me?_____

_____

_____

_____

7 Keeping a Journal
Nature Notes II

What You'll LEARN
Look at the notes you've taken after observing your place in nature for several weeks. You can use those notes to reach conclusions, or explanations, based on your observations.

What You'll DO
Read the notes you've taken over the last six weeks about the place in nature you were watching.

What You'll WRITE
Answer the questions below. Remember to use precise words to describe what you have observed.

1. Did the kinds of plants you saw change? Can you draw a conclusion about why they did or did not change? _____

_____

_____

_____

_____

2. Did the condition of the plants change? If so, draw a conclusion about why this happened. _____

_____

_____

_____

_____

3. Did the kinds or numbers of animals you saw change? How? Draw a conclusion about why they did or did not change. _____

_____

_____

_____

_____

_____

4. How has the weather changed during the last six weeks? _____

_____

_____

_____

5. Draw a conclusion about whether a change in season has affected the living things in the spot you chose. _____

_____

_____

_____

6. What other changes have you seen in the spot you have been watching? _____

_____

_____

_____

7. Draw a conclusion about the reasons behind the changes you saw. _____

_____

_____

_____

8. What conclusions can you draw about the impact that people have had on this area in the past six weeks? _____

_____

_____

_____

9. What conclusions can you draw about why the condition of this area has changed?

_____

_____

_____

10. Draw a conclusion about how this area will change in the next six weeks. _____

_____

_____

_____

_____

LESSON 8 Making Inferences
What Do You See?

What You'll LEARN
By closely observing these before-and-after pictures of a dangerous storm, you will be able to make inferences—good, logical guesses based on what you already know—about what happened.

What You'll DO
These photographs of the same place were taken just before and after a terrible storm in 1992. Observe the differences in the two photographs carefully.

What You'll WRITE

After you have studied the photographs, answer the questions below.

1. Make an inference about the destruction that occurred in this storm. _____

_____

_____

_____

_____

2. From what you see in these pictures, make an inference about where this storm took place. Why do you think this? _____

_____

_____

_____

_____

3. What kind of storm do you think this might have been? Make an inference that explains your answer. _____

_____

_____

_____

_____

4. Do you think this storm might have resulted in loss of life? Infer why. _____

_____

_____

_____

_____

5. Think about what you see in these photographs. What would you tell someone who was planning to build a new building on this site and wanted to protect the building from future storms like this one? _____

_____

_____

_____

_____

_____

LESSON 9
Analyzing Information
Creating a Bar Graph

What You'll LEARN

By sorting and classifying raw information, you can create a bar graph that organizes information visually. A bar graph is often used when people want to compare things. After you have built the graph, you can write a caption for the graph that explains it.

Here is an example of a bar graph. In this case, the information is shown as a series of horizontal bars. Bar graphs can also be constructed so that the information runs vertically. In this bar graph, the bottom line, or axis, lists the average miles per gallon. The vertical axis lists types of vehicles.

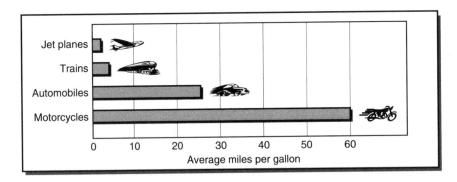

When you look at this bar graph, it is easy to compare the miles per gallon that each of these vehicles gets.

What You'll DO

You are a newspaper reporter writing a story about the recycling programs in several local towns that are all about the same size. Below is the information you gathered from each town on its weekly recycling program.

CRAWFORD
1.7 tons newspaper
no glass
no plastic
300 lbs. aluminum

ST. JEAN
300 lbs. glass
1 ton newspaper
80 lbs. plastic
500 lbs. aluminum

MORGAN
2.2 tons newspaper
550 lbs. aluminum
590 lbs. glass
no plastic

What You'll WRITE

1. Use this space to create a bar graph that displays the information from the three towns.

2. What did you learn from this graph about the recycling programs in the three towns ?

_____

_____

_____

_____

3. The bar graph will illustrate a front-page story on the topic. The headline will read: "A Tale of Three Towns' Trash." You know readers will probably first read the headline. Then they will look at the graph. Finally, they will look at the caption under the graph. Write the caption that will go underneath the graph. Use what you learned from the graph to write a caption that explains the bar graph.

Caption: _____

_____

_____

_____

_____

_____

LESSON 10 Experimenting
Forming a Hypothesis

What You'll LEARN
One of the foundations of science is being able to create an experiment to test a hypothesis. You'll learn how to write a hypothesis on these pages.

What You'll DO
A *hypothesis* is a guess that answers a question. A scientist will wonder why something happens or how it happens and ask a question.

Asking the right question is important if you want an answer you can use. Stay away from asking questions that are too broad, cannot be answered except by very sophisticated equipment, or are unanswerable. These will lead to useless experiments. For example, a student whose question is "What materials is the planet Venus composed of?" will not be able to create an experiment to prove his guess.

Some of the best science questions come from wondering about what we see around us. For example, a student might want to find out whether expensive dog food makes her dog look and feel better than the less expensive kind. Another student might want to discover whether she can train herself to wake up without an alarm clock.

What You'll WRITE
List some science questions you would like to answer.

1. _____

_____

2. _____

_____

3. _____

_____

4. _____

_____

5. _____

_____

Now, choose one question to answer. Base your choice on which question most interests you and which you think you could design an experiment to answer.

The next step is forming a hypothesis, or a possible answer to the question. A hypothesis is always a statement. You form a hypothesis by observing and then thinking of an explanation. After you have a hypothesis, you test, or experiment, to find out if your hypothesis is right. You can make a better hypothesis by finding out more about your subject.

Here is one example of a question and a possible hypothesis.

Question: What liquid will help plants grow the best: orange soda, coffee, water, or orange juice?

Hypothesis: Water will help plants grow the best.

Write hypotheses that could answer the questions you asked in numbers 1–5 on the previous page. Then choose the hypothesis you think is most likely to answer your question. Circle the hypothesis you will test.

6. _____

_____

_____

_____

7. _____

_____

_____

_____

_____

8. _____

_____

_____

_____

_____

9. _____

_____

_____

_____

10. _____

_____

_____

_____

LESSON 11 Experimenting
Testing a Hypothesis

What You'll LEARN

Once you have decided which hypothesis you want to test, you'll need to design a way to test it. An experiment is the way you test the hypothesis.

There are two kinds of traits that a hypothesis may have:

1. traits that can be measured, such as the speed of a car

2. traits that must be compared to be understood, such as the amount of growth in plants that are given different fertilizers

A hypothesis may be difficult to test if it is worded unclearly or if it is too broad. It may also be difficult to test if the results are based on traits that are subjective, or based on opinion. For example, you cannot test to see if something is beautiful.

What You'll DO

You must be able to test a hypothesis. Below are four hypotheses. Decide on a way to test each. If the hypothesis would be difficult to test, write why.

Hypothesis	How you test it
1. People would rather eat sweet flavors than salty flavors.	
2. Sugar dissolves faster in hot water than in cold water.	
3. Plastic grocery bags are stronger than paper grocery bags.	
4. Dogs are friendlier than cats.	

What You'll WRITE Answer these questions about the hypothesis you decided to test in Lesson 10, Experimenting: Forming a Hypothesis.

1. Write your hypothesis here. _____

_____

_____

_____

_____

_____

2. Write three ways you could test your hypothesis.

a. _____

_____

_____

_____

_____

b. _____

_____

_____

_____

_____

_____

c. _____

_____

_____

_____

_____

3. Which way do you think will lead to the most accurate and measurable results? Why?

_____

_____

_____

_____

_____

_____

12 Experimenting
LESSON
Designing the Experiment

What You'll LEARN

Making assumptions about what you will be testing is one part of designing the experiment. Variables and controls are important in making sure that an experiment succeeds. Keeping good notes of your work is also important.

What You'll DO

As you set up the experiment, you will first need to identify your assumptions. For example, if you are doing an experiment about garden plants, you assume, or take for granted, that they need sunlight to make food.

You will also need to identify the variables in your experiment and set up controls. A *variable* is something within an experiment that can be changed. For example, if you were doing an experiment to see what kind of fertilizer works best, you would give the plants different fertilizers.

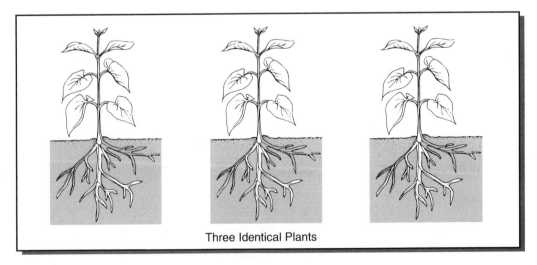
Three Identical Plants

A *control* is something that does not change. In an experiment about how plants grow with different kinds of fertilizer, you would grow one plant with no fertilizer. This would be your control. That way, you could compare your results.

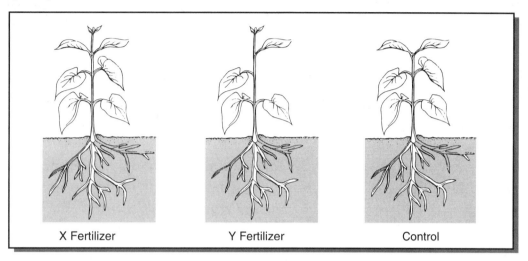

X Fertilizer   Y Fertilizer   Control

What You'll WRITE

1. What assumptions are you making as you design your experiment? _____

_____

_____

_____

2. Do you need variables in your experiment? Why or why not? What variables will you use?

_____

_____

_____

_____

_____

3. Do you need a control in your experiment? Why or why not? If you need a control, how will you set it up? _____

_____

_____

_____

_____

The last thing you need to do is set up a way to record your results. You should take notes about what your experiment shows. Keep track of your results in your science notebook or on a separate piece of paper.

Now you are almost ready to conduct your experiment.

13 Experimenting Analyzing Data

LESSON

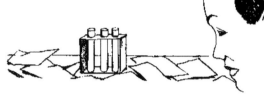

What You'll LEARN
Once you have collected all your data, or information, you need to analyze it to find out if it proves your hypothesis or not.

What You'll DO
When you analyze data from an experiment, you judge whether it supports your hypothesis. Review the data you collected in Lesson 12, Experimenting: Designing the Experiment. Use these results to decide if this data supports your hypothesis.

What You'll WRITE

1. Write a sentence that describes the data you collected in your experiment.

_____

_____

2. Look at your hypothesis again. Did the data you collected in your experiment support your hypothesis? Explain why or why not. _____

_____

_____

_____

_____

3. What did you learn from this experiment? _____

_____

_____

_____

_____

4. What would you do differently if you wanted to do the same experiment again?

_____

_____

_____

_____

14 Presenting Information An Oral Report

LESSON

What You'll LEARN Presenting information in a speech or oral report is a useful skill not only for school, but also for work. These pages will give you practice in putting together an oral report.

What You'll DO Choose a science topic to learn more about. Then organize the information you learn and write it into a report to present. Because this is a science report, you must remember to define science words and ideas that your audience may not know.

What You'll WRITE The easiest way to do an oral report is to break it into smaller pieces and accomplish them one at a time.

1. **Select and limit a topic.** Choose something that you are interested in. Make sure that you can find out enough information to make a good report. Stay away from topics that are too broad or too narrow. For example, the subject of mammals is too large to cover easily, but a report on zebras would be manageable.

   Topics in which I am interested: _____

   _____

   _____

   _____

   _____

2. **Collect information.** Use the same sources for an oral report as for a written one—books, newspapers, magazine articles. You can also interview people for information. (See Writing a Report: Choosing a Topic, in Lesson 15, on page 30.)

   Sources for information (be specific: list specific books and magazine articles):

   _____

   _____

   _____

   _____

3. **Plan your report.** There are several ways to present information in an oral report.

    If you are demonstrating something (for example, if you invented a new electrical switch and are explaining how it works), present your speech in a series of steps.

    If you are writing a speech to convince your audience, state the problem, list possible solutions, and then argue for the solution you think is the best.

    If you are making an oral report on information you learned about a topic, present it as if it were a written report, with an introduction, sections that explain main ideas, and details that support each section.

    How will you organize your speech, and why? _____

    _____

    _____

    _____

4. **Plan your introduction.** In an oral report, the introduction is important. During the first sentences you speak, most of your audience will decide whether to listen to you or not. You might want to find an interesting or startling fact to begin your report. You can engage the audience by asking a question. You can also get the audience's attention by talking about something related to the topic that happened to you.

    Write your introduction here. _____

    _____

    _____

    _____

    _____

    _____

5. **Write the body of your oral report.** After you have introduced your topic, you need to let the audience know what you are going to talk about. After you have stated that, you can use words like these to signal your audience so it will know what to listen for.

    "I want to tell you about . . ."
    "There are three points I want to make . . ."
    "Here is an example of . . ."

Organize the body of your report so that you cover all the points that you want to make. Write an outline here. _____

_____

_____

_____

_____

_____

6. **Conclude your oral report.** Your conclusion will depend on how you organized your report.

   If your report featured a demonstration, you can end your speech by summarizing the steps you used and then showing the results of the demonstration.

   If your report was a speech to convince, go through your arguments again briefly. End with a strong statement about why your position is right.

   If your report is an informative speech, summarize and review your main points.

Write your conclusion here. _____

_____

_____

_____

_____

_____

_____

Transfer the main points of your introduction, body, and conclusion to index cards—one point per card. Use these as cue cards when presenting your report.

As you practice your oral report, go over this checklist:

☐ Are my notes prepared on cards so that I can read them easily?

☐ Do I use my voice to emphasize the main points I want to make?

☐ Have I practiced using gestures to help make my points?

☐ Am I speaking clearly and slowly?

15 Writing a Report
Choosing a Topic

What You'll LEARN You will learn how to decide on a topic for a science report that is broad enough to be interesting but narrow enough to be done.

What You'll DO Read how one student decided on a science report topic.

1. She knew that she was interested in writing about the oceans.

2. She researched the topic. She found out that whole books had been written about oceans, so the topic was too broad.

3. She thought about what she was interested in about the oceans and came up with these ideas: Sea animals, whales, whether whales are endangered, and how much intelligence whales have.

4. She went to the library. She found out that there was too much information about some of her possible topics, and too little information about others. She chose the topic "Are whales endangered?" for her report.

What You'll WRITE Answer these questions to help you decide on a topic.

1. What general topics am I interested in?

   a. _____

   b. _____

   c. _____

   d. _____

2. Which topic am I most interested in? Why? _____

   _____

   _____

   _____

   _____

   _____

   _____

3. How can I narrow this topic so that I will be able to write a research paper about it? (Go to the library to find out what information there is about your topic in books and magazines.)

a. _____

b. _____

c. _____

4. Choose the narrow topic that most interests you: _____

5. Begin your research by listing books and magazine articles you will use as sources for your report. These sources are called the *bibliography*. If you will be using the *Readers' Guide to Periodical Literature*, follow these steps:

a. The *Guides* are listed by year. Check the years in which you think your subject may be mentioned.

b. Subjects are listed alphabetically. If there are no entries, try a related subject.

c. If the listing for your subject says *See* _____, look under the other term. If there are subheadings, look under the one closest to your topic.

d. Here is a typical entry with its parts explained:

subject — **SPACE RESEARCH** Back to the — article title
future (meaning of successful — article description
illustrations — Discovery launch) M.D. Lemonick. — author
il *Discover* 10:42–3+ Ja '89
magazine title

volume   pages   date

6. What are the three best sources for the information you want to include in your report? List each book or magazine title, the book's publisher or author, the magazine and date if from a magazine, and the pages the information is on.

_____

_____

_____

_____

16 LESSON Writing a Report
Taking Notes

What You'll LEARN   It's important to keep track of the information you're learning for your science report. You'll also learn how you can take notes you can later use to write your report.

What You'll DO   The easiest way to write a science report is to begin by organizing the information you are learning. Taking good notes is important. If you don't, researching and writing a report can seem overwhelming.

What You'll WRITE   By answering the questions in this lesson, you will have outlined information from your first article or book. You can then use this information to help you write your report.

1. What questions do you want to answer in your report? _____

_____

_____

_____

You can use a notebook to write information for your report. Some writers find that taking notes on 3-inch by 5-inch cards is helpful. By doing this, they are able to put the cards in the order in which they want to use them when they write their report.

Writers who use this method often write a heading on the card to help them sort the cards later. Here is one student's example:

results of whaling   Jamison,
                          "Whales"

Because of so much whaling over the years,
some species may already be extinct.
"If unregulated whaling continues, more
species will become extinct." (p. 10)

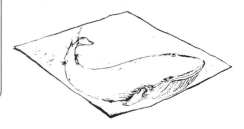

2. Skim the article or book. All of it may have to do with your topic. Maybe only part of the material has something to do with your topic, though. When you have read what you need to, write the name of the book or article, the pages that were helpful, and then, briefly, write what you have learned that helps you answer your question.

_____

_____

_____

_____

_____

_____

_____

_____

3. What evidence or examples does the author give to back up what he or she is writing?

_____

_____

_____

_____

_____

_____

_____

4. If an author writes an opinion that you want to include in your report, write it here exactly. Put quotation marks around the author's words. Also write the page on which the quotation appeared and who said it if the speaker was someone other than the author.

_____

_____

_____

_____

_____

_____

_____

17 Writing a Report
Creating an Outline

What You'll LEARN

Notes for a report need to be organized into an outline. In an outline, you write phrases that explain the main points of your report. From that, you can write a first draft.

Looking at all the notes you've made for a science report can be discouraging. How can you organize them into a report so that they make sense?

What You'll DO

The first step is to read all the information you collected. After that, sort the information into piles with similar main ideas. By then, you'll have a start on organizing your report.

What You'll WRITE

Answer these questions to get the outline started.

1. Look at one of the piles. Write a sentence that describes its general topic.

_____

_____

_____

2. Do the same thing for all the piles you made. On another piece of paper, write a topic sentence that describes each pile.

Now sort each pile into smaller groups by idea. For example, if the pile contains notes about the effects of pollution on whales, the smaller groups might be (a) what pollution does to whales' food sources; (b) how pollution affects the breeding grounds of whales; and (c) how pollution can cause whales to become diseased.

3. Write the ideas in one of your piles here. Then use another piece of paper to make a list for each pile. _____

_____

_____

_____

Now you can create an outline. At the top, write the statement that describes what your report is about. Next, put the groups in order in a way that supports the topic of your paper. Write a main point for each of these groups. Under each of these, write phrases that support each main point.

Here is one student's outline:

Statement: Whales are an endangered species, but
we can help keep them from becoming extinct.

I. Introduction
II. Threats to whales
    A. Commercial whaling
    B. Pollution
    C. Disturbing their habitat

III. What we can do to help save whales
    A. Stop or regulate whaling
    B. Stop polluting the waters where whales live
    C. Ban people from whale breeding grounds
IV. Conclusion

4. Use this space to write your own outline, or use a separate piece of paper.

Statement: _____

_____

 I. Introduction: _____

_____

_____

II. _____
    A. _____
    B. _____

III. _____
    A. _____
    B. _____

IV. Conclusion: _____

_____

_____

18 Writing a Report
LESSON 18 The First Draft

What You'll LEARN You will learn to use your outline and notes to write a draft of your science report.

What You'll DO Write your first draft.

What You'll WRITE Answer the questions on these pages to help you write your first draft.

The introduction. In a science report, this is the first paragraph. In the introduction, you include the sentence that explains what the report is about.

Here is one student's introduction:

> Even though whales are probably the largest animals that have ever lived, they are still in trouble. About half of the species of whales are rare. Of the whales that have been hunted, almost all are endangered. Also, people threaten the whale with pollution and by disturbing the places whales live. If humans want to, though, there is still time to protect these unusual, beautiful creatures.

1. Use this space to write an introduction to your report. _____

_____

_____

_____

_____

_____

The body. For the main part of your report, or the body, it is useful to have your outline and notecards at hand. As you begin to write, follow your outline. Use the notes you made to help you write.

As you make each point on your outline, make sure to include a topic sentence that explains your point. For example, if you were going to write the body of the report about whales, this might be the topic sentence about one section:

Many species of whales—the blue, sei, Bryde's fin, bowhead, humpback, and right—have become endangered because of whaling.

2. Write the topic sentence for the first point you will be making. _____

_____

_____

_____

Follow your topic sentence with evidence from your notes to back up your topic sentence. For example, the sentence above might be followed with information about how long whaling has been going on and how the numbers of whales have gone down since.

Conclusion. When you have made all the points you want to make in the body of your report, write the concluding paragraph. In this paragraph, you summarize what you have shown in the paper. Here is the student conclusion to the report about whales:

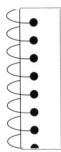

There are still threats to whales by countries that do not agree with restrictions on whaling. Whales also face increasing environmental dangers as populations of humans grow. If the people of the world decide to keep whales from extinction, though, it is not too late to save the whales.

3. Write your conclusion. _____

_____

_____

_____

_____

19 Writing a Report
LESSON
Revising and Footnotes

What You'll LEARN   Revising your work and writing the footnotes and bibliography are the final steps in creating a science report.

What You'll DO   By *revising* the draft, you have a chance to polish your work. Use this checklist to make your science report better.

- ☐ Does your draft match your outline?

- ☐ Does the writing make sense? Does one point lead to the next?

- ☐ Have you chosen the right words to say exactly what you mean?

- ☐ Have you checked the grammar in the report?

- ☐ Have you proofread the report for spelling, capitalization, and punctuation?

Footnotes give credit to the writers whose ideas you are using in your report. They also give readers the ability to find out more if they want to or to check your sources to see if you understood the writer. You use footnotes when you:

quote an author exactly
use a writer's ideas
use numbers or statistics

Footnotes can either be listed at the end of your report or at the bottom of the page on which the footnote appears. They are usually numbered in order throughout the report. Here are the forms for different kinds of footnote sources:

A book:
[1] Jane Meehan, <u>Whales and Their Habitat</u> (New York: Shanan Press, 1996), p. 39.

A magazine article:
[2] Peter B. Neir, "The Trouble with Whaling," <u>Environmental News</u>, March 1995, p. 22.

A newspaper article:
[3] "New Hope for Blue Whales," by Kelcy Argo, <u>Bedford Chronicle</u>, July 17, 1993.

An article from an encyclopedia:
[4] "Whales," <u>The Concise Columbia Encyclopedia</u>, 1983 ed., p. 917.

If you use the same source more than once, you don't have to write all the information again. Instead, write:

[5] Neir, p. 25.

The *bibliography* belongs at the end of your report. In the bibliography, you will list the sources you used for your report in alphabetical order. Here is a sample bibliography entry:

Argo, Kelcy. "New Hope for Blue Whales," <u>Bedford Chronicle</u>, July 17, 1993.

Revise the draft and prepare the footnotes and bibliography. Go over the draft of your report and revise it. Use the checklist on page 38 as a guide.

What You'll WRITE

1. Write the first footnote for your science report. _____

_____

_____

2. Write your bibliography here. _____

_____

_____

_____

_____

_____

_____

Make a final copy of your report on a separate sheet of paper.

20 Writing a Report
LESSON Creating an Essay Test

What You'll LEARN Essay tests are a part of life. You can learn how to do them from the inside out—by writing your own.

What You'll DO You'll create an essay test based on the science report that you wrote in Lessons 15–19. Here are some things to think about as you write your essay test. Remember, you're not thinking like a student now—you're thinking like a teacher.

1. Teachers often want to see if students understand the main point of the writing. You can do that by creating an essay question that asks for exactly that.

2. Another way to find out if a student understands what he or she has read is to have the student summarize the reading. This gives the teacher a sense of whether the student understands the main points.

3. An essay question may ask for examples that supports a main point. This shows the teacher that the student is paying attention to the details.

4. Essay questions may also ask students to go beyond the information in the report, and draw conclusions, make inferences, or predict outcomes. By doing this, students prove that they can think beyond what's on the page.

5. You have probably noticed that essay tests tend to proceed in order, from the easiest to the most difficult questions. This can help students to focus and lead them to handle more difficult skills.

6. *Code Words:* When teachers use certain words in essay tests, they have something specific in mind. Here is how to decode essay test words:

Code Words	Meanings
describe means to	give details
explain means to	give the reasons
summarize means to	state the main points briefly
compare means to	mention similarities
contrast means to	mention differences
illustrate means to	give examples
discuss means to	think about all the angles of a topic
list means to	do exactly that—no details

What You'll WRITE

Write five essay questions about your report on the lines below. Make sure that your questions will show that your "student" knows the report's main points and details. Write a question that will show that your student understands the importance of the information in your report. Also include a question that shows that your student sees the implications of what you wrote. Don't forget to include the answers to your questions.

1. _____

_____

_____

_____

_____

2. _____

_____

_____

_____

_____

3. _____

_____

_____

_____

_____

4. _____

_____

_____

_____

_____

5. _____

_____

_____

_____

_____

21 Experimenting
LESSON
Testing Cleaning Products

What You'll LEARN

Many cleaning products claim they can clean better than the competition. Are their claims true? Are you better off just using plain soap and water instead? You can design an experiment to find out.

What You'll DO

Your school spends a lot of money every week to clean walls, floors, and countertops. What kind of cleaner works best? Construct an experiment to test several different cleaning products on different kinds of grime. Test grease, dirt, chocolate, and crayon. Answer these questions to help you set up the experiment. If you need more information about experimenting, see pages 20–27.

What You'll WRITE

1. What is the question you want to answer? _____

_____

_____

2. What hypothesis will you be testing in the experiment? _____

_____

_____

3. What are the variables in this experiment? _____

_____

_____

4. What are the controls? _____

_____

_____

5. Describe how you will set up the experiment.

_____

_____

_____

_____

Fill in this chart to keep track of your results, or create one like it on another piece of paper. The top row can be the list of products, and the left column can be the kind of grime you tried to remove. In the last column, you can write notes about the results.

6. Analyze the information you collected. Then write a recommendation for the school custodian about the kind of product that should be used. You could also recommend two or more products if a kind of cleaner does a particularly good job on one kind of dirt.

_____

_____

_____

_____

_____

_____

_____

_____

_____

_____

_____

_____

22 Investigating an Ad Fact or Opinion?

LESSON

What You'll LEARN
Are the claims made by manufacturers based on science? In this exercise, you'll take a look at boasts for products.

What You'll DO
Look through magazines for an ad for a diet product. You will be reading this ad to see how it sells its product. You will need to tell the difference between fact and opinion. "Miracle Diet is great!" is an opinion. Information on a weight-loss experiment from an outside agency, like the American Medical Association, is more likely to be a provable fact.

What You'll WRITE
Answer these questions about the advertisement. Then write a letter to a friend who wants to know whether to buy the product or not.

1. What opinions, if any, are in the ad? How can you tell they are opinions?

_____

_____

2. What facts, if any, are in the ad? How can you tell they are facts?

_____

_____

3. Why do you think the writer of the ad wrote it the way he did? What was he trying to accomplish?_____

_____

_____

4. Who is this ad written to appeal to? How can you tell? _____

_____

_____

5. What information is not included in the ad that might be important for a buyer to know?_____

_____

_____

6. Write a letter to a friend who has asked you for advice about the product in the ad. He wants to know if you would recommend using this product. In your letter, be sure to explain what opinions and facts in the ad led you to your recommendation.

Dear _____,

_____

_____

_____

_____

_____

_____

_____

_____

_____

_____

_____

_____

_____

_____

_____

_____

_____

_____

_____

_____

_____

_____

_____

_____

23
Comparing Data
Choosing a Snack

What You'll LEARN You might be able to read a nutrition label, but can you compare and contrast several labels and choose the most healthful food?

What You'll DO Study these three food labels. Each is from a snack that a day camp is considering buying for its program. The camp wants the most healthful food. You must compare (look for similarities) and contrast (look for differences) these foods and come up with a recommendation. Then you have to explain your choice to the camp director.

Nutrition Facts
Serving Size 1 Cookie (15 g)
Serving Per Container 12

Amount Per Serving

Calories 50 Calories from Fat 0

	% Daily Valve*
Total Fat 0g	**0%**
Saturated Fat 0g	**0%**
Ployunsaturated Fat 0g	
Monounsaturated Fat 0g	
Cholesterol 0mg	**0%**
Sodium 65mg	**3%**
Total Carbohydrate 12g	**4%**
Dietary Fiber Less than 1g	**1%**
Sugars 7g	
Protein 1g	

Vitamin A 0%	•	Vitamin C 0%
Calcium 0%	•	Iron 2%

* Percent Daily Values are based on a 2,000 calorie diet. Your daily values may be higher or lower depending on your calorie needs:

	Calories:	2,000	2,500
Total Fat	Less than	65g	80g
Sat Fat	Less than	20g	25g
Cholesterol	Less than	300mg	300mg
Soduim	Less than	2400mg	2400mg
Total Carbohydrate		300g	375g
Dietary Fiber		25g	30g

Calories per gram: Fat 9 • Carbohydrate 4 • Protein 4

Nutrition Facts
Serving Size 1 tart (48 g)
Serving Per Container 8

Amount Per Serving

Calories 190 Calories from Fat 45

	% Daily Valve*
Total Fat 5g	**8%**
Saturated Fat 1.5g	**7%**
Cholesterol 0mg	**0%**
Sodium 190mg	**8%**
Total Carbohydrate 35g	**12%**
Dietary Fiber 1g	**3%**
Sugars 17g	
Protein 2g	

Vitamin A 10% • Vitamin C 0% • Calcium 0% • Iron 10%

Thiamin 10% • Riboflavin 10% • Niacin 10% • Vitamin B$_6$ 10%

* Percent Daily Values are based on a 2,000 calorie diet. Your daily values may be higher or lower depending on your calorie needs:

	Calories:	2,000	2,500
Total Fat	Less than	65g	80g
Sat Fat	Less than	20g	25g
Cholesterol	Less than	300mg	300mg
Soduim	Less than	2400mg	2400mg
Total Carbohydrate		300g	375mg
Dietary Fiber		25g	30g

Nutrition Facts
Serving Size 1 Bar (37 g)

Amount/serving, % DV*
Total Fat 3.0g, 5% • Sat. Fat 0.5g, 3% • **Cholest.** 0mg, 0% • **Sodium** 60mg, 3% • **Total Carb.** 27g, 9% • Fiber 1g, 4% • Sugars 12g • Protein 2g
Vitamin A 15% • Vitamin C 0% • Calcium 0% • Iron 10% • Thiamin 25% • Riboflavin 25% • Niacin 25% • Vitamin B$_6$ 25% • Folate 25% • Phosphorus 4% • Magnesium 2% • Zinc 10%

To help you compare and contrast these foods, create a bar graph on a separate piece of paper. The bar graph should include the information that will help you understand the foods' healthfulness, such as fat, sugars, and vitamins. If you need help making a bar graph, see Analyzing Information: Creating a Bar Graph, in Lesson 9, on page 18.

What You'll WRITE

Use the graph you made to help you answer these questions about the labels. Use complete sentences. Then write a memo to the camp director recommending one, two, three, or none of the snack foods whose labels are on this page 46.

1. Compare the percentage of fat in each snack. _____

_____

_____

_____

_____

2. Which of the snacks has the most vitamins and minerals? How do the others compare?

_____

_____

_____

3. Which do you think is the least healthful snack? Why? _____

_____

_____

4. Write a memo to the camp director comparing and contrasting these snacks and explaining which, if any, you would recommend be served to the day campers. Explain your reasons. _____

_____

_____

_____

_____

_____

_____

_____

_____

_____

_____

_____

_____

_____

_____

24 Experimenting
Are Horoscopes Accurate?

LESSON

What You'll LEARN
Can you believe everything you read—particularly in the astrology column of the newspaper? Find out by designing an experiment.

What You'll DO
You're a television reporter. Your producer wants to run a story about horoscopes: Do they really predict the future? He's told you to find out and then write a story for broadcast about what you learn.

You need to design an experiment to find out how accurate the horoscopes in the daily paper are. (If you want more information about experimenting, see Lessons 10–13, on pages 20–27.)

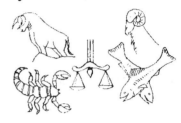

What You'll WRITE
Answer these questions to help you design your experiment.

1. What question do you want to answer? _____

_____

_____

2. What is your hypothesis or your best guess at the answer to the question?

_____

_____

_____

3. Write the best way to test your hypothesis. _____

_____

_____

_____

_____

_____

_____

_____

_____

_____

_____

Conduct your experiment. Keep careful records of what you learn.

4. What were the results of your experiment? _____

_____

_____

_____

_____

_____

5. Did your experiment prove or disprove your hypothesis? Explain. _____

_____

_____

_____

_____

_____

_____

6. Now write a script based on what you learned. As you write, remember the 5Ws: Who, What, When, Where, and Why.

_____

_____

_____

_____

_____

_____

_____

_____

_____

_____

_____

_____

_____

_____

25 Analyzing a Chart
LESSON
Can You Trust Forecasts?

What You'll LEARN

Can you trust the weather report? Many businesses must know what the weather will be. You can analyze the newspaper report and find out if you can trust it to predict the weather.

What You'll DO

Imagine that you work for a construction company. The boss is sure that she can't trust the weekly weather reports in the paper, and she wants to hire a private forecasting service. Your job is to find out if the weather reports are reliable.

You have to collect data, or information, to do your job. Pick up a copy of the newspaper, and fill in the chart with the predicted weather for the week. The next day, begin to keep daily records in your chart. Use the newspaper from the next day to record the actual high and low temperatures.

	Mon.	Tues.	Wed.	Thurs.	Fri.
Predicted high temp.					
Actual high temp.					
Predicted low temp.					
Actual low temp.					
Predicted conditions					
Actual conditions					

You've got all the data on the weather for the week. Now you have to analyze it and give your boss a recommendation. Your first step should be to create a graph on a separate piece of paper so that you can understand the information more easily. If you need help making a graph, see Analyzing Information: Creating a Bar Graph, in Lesson 9, on page 18.

What You'll WRITE

Should your boss hire a private service or trust the weekly weather predictions in the newspaper? Write a memo that she can use to make her decision. Analyze the data for her and make a recommendation. When you analyze data, you look at how different pieces of information fit together to form patterns. For example, you would want to analyze the data to see if the predicted low and high temperatures were right.

MEMO

To: _____

From: _____

Subject: _____

Date: _____

_____

_____

_____

_____

_____

_____

_____

_____

_____

_____

_____

_____

_____

_____

_____

_____

_____

_____

_____

_____

26
LESSON

Predicting Outcomes
What Happens Next?

What You'll LEARN
When you predict an outcome in science, you are making an educated guess based on what you know. Practice in predicting can help you make decisions in everyday life.

What You'll DO
Read this newspaper article about a predicted flash flood. Think about what you know about flash floods. If you wish, research what happens during a flash flood.

RAPAHONK, Oregon—Local police officers spent most of the day in Thursday's rainstorm trying to convince Leonora and George Handon to come out into the rain.

"I don't care what you say. I'm not moving," 54-year-old Leonora Handon told officer Jeff Wilson as he pleaded with her to leave her home on the edge of a swollen creek.

"I've been here for 35 years, and nothing's ever happened. I'm not leaving now," Handon's husband George told Wilson, who had spent the last hour trying to convince the Handons to move to safety.

"This is the most stubborn couple I've ever met," Wilson said. "That doesn't matter. What matters is that unless they move, they might die when that flash flood comes roaring by."

Wilson, along with other Rapahonk police and fire officers, spent most of yesterday telling residents of Wold Creek's banks of the danger of flash flooding. After two solid weeks of rain, the creek's waters are dangerously high. Officials warned that one more day of rain could cause a flash flood that would destroy houses up and down the creek.

There is more rain forecast for tomorrow. The Handons refuse to leave.

What You'll WRITE Predict what happened the next day after the rain storm. Use what you learned in the article and what you know about flash floods. Then imagine you are the reporter sent out to write a news story on the rain storm. What happened? What did you see? As you plan the article, answer these five questions:

1. Who? _____

2. What? _____

_____

3. When? _____

4. Where? _____

5. Why? _____

_____

6. Now write your story. Remember to use clear, descriptive language that explains clearly what happened and why it is important.

_____

_____

_____

_____

_____

_____

_____

_____

_____

_____

_____

_____

_____

_____

_____

_____

_____

27 Explaining Science
How Does This Work?

LESSON 27

What You'll LEARN

We are often faced with machines that we have to use and understand. Explaining a scientific principle so that everyone can understand it can be tricky.

What You'll DO

Below are three items based on scientific principles. Choose one and write a description of how and why it works. Describe and explain the science behind the item (you may have to use references to understand it). Your description will be included in the instructions that are sold with the item.

Remember that when you explain science to nonscientists, you try to use language that is as clear and simple as possible. You should also avoid scientific terms, unless you explain them.

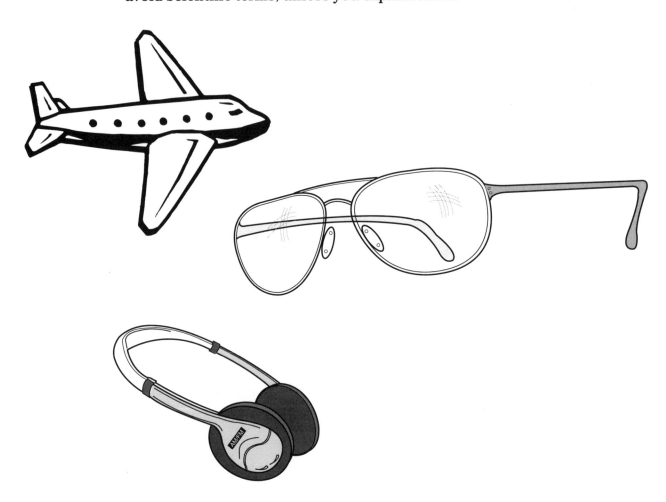

What You'll WRITE Here's a sample brochure for a camera. Use it to help you start writing your own brochure for one of the three machines pictured on page 54.

GLOBE CAMERA, INC.

What You Need to Know About Your New Camera

Note: This equipment has been tested and found to be complete and within the limits of a Class B digital device, pursuant to publication 15 the FCC Rules.

Write the copy (the words) that will appear in the brochure that comes with the item you are writing about. You need to explain how and why it works, including the scientific principle behind the item. You are writing for a general audience that wants to understand how the item works.

What You Need to Know About Your New _____

_____

_____

_____

_____

_____

_____

_____

_____

_____

_____

_____

_____

_____

_____

_____

_____

_____

28 An Essay Contest
Scientist for a Day

What You'll LEARN

Answering an essay question is a fine art. On these pages, you'll get some practice.

What You'll DO

A local university is running an essay contest. The student who wins will be able to spend a day with the scientist of his or her choice.

Here are a few tips for answering essay questions:

1. Read the directions carefully. Sometimes, essay questions ask for more than one thing. You may have to both provide an example and give details.

2. Write a rough outline for your answer. What are the main points you want to cover? What details support each point?

3. Make your answer concise. Use precise language that supports what you have to say.

4. Science essay questions often require facts and evidence. If you are writing an essay test about a novel, you are more likely to be asked to argue a point of view or justify your opinion.

5. Double-check grammar, spelling, and punctuation.

What You'll WRITE

Answer these essay questions. You will probably want to do some research to be able to answer them well.

1. What kind of science most interests you? Why? _____

_____

_____

_____

_____

_____

2. How do you think this branch of science benefits humanity? Give three examples.

_____

_____

_____

_____

_____

3. Write what you think you would be doing during a workday if you worked in this branch of science. _____

_____

_____

_____

_____

_____

_____

4. What would you like to accomplish if you worked in this branch of science?

_____

_____

_____

_____

_____

_____

_____

20 Gathering Data
LESSON
Designing a Survey

What You'll LEARN

Companies design surveys to find out what the public thinks about an issue. In this exercise, you will design a public-attitude survey and then analyze the answers you get.

What You'll DO

Designing a public-attitude survey involves writing questions that help you gather information, or data, that you can then analyze. One example is whether nuclear energy is good or bad. Choose a science issue that people disagree about. Then design a public-attitude survey that will show where people stand on the issue. Here are some guidelines to use in designing your survey:

1. **Narrow your topic.** If it is too broad, you will get answers that are too broad in return. For example, if you ask questions about whether people do or do not like pollution, you will get predictable answers that do not help you understand a specific situation.

2. **Avoid bias.** Bias, or prejudice, can make your survey inaccurate. To make sure this doesn't happen, write your questions so they are neutral and do not show how you feel about the topic. For example, if you ask "Don't you think nuclear energy is a bad thing?" the answers you get might not reflect how people really feel.

3. **Narrow your questions.** In most cases, giving people questions that are too open-ended will not allow you to compare opinions but only to gather them. An example of an open-ended question is: "How do you feel about pollution?" Instead, ask yes or no questions. Then you will be able to count the answers more easily.

Here is one survey a student wrote to help her find out what people would do to reduce air pollution.

PUBLIC OPINION SURVEY

Hello, my name is _____ . I am a student at _____ school. My class is gathering information about the issue of _____ . Would you share with me how you feel about it?

If "No," say thank you. If "Yes," continue.

1. In your opinion, is air pollution a health problem in our city?

                     YES   NO   UNDECIDED

2. Would you be willing to use your car less in order to reduce air pollution?

                     YES   NO   UNDECIDED

3. Would you be willing to stop using your backyard barbecue in order to reduce air pollution?

                     YES   NO   UNDECIDED

What You'll Use this page to work on your survey.
WRITE

1. What topic do you want to gather information about? _____

_____

2. What questions could you ask to find out public opinion on this issue?

a. _____

_____

b. _____

_____

c. _____

_____

d. _____

_____

Use this checklist to think about the survey you designed.

☐ Are the questions you wrote free of bias?

☐ Are the questions easy for people to understand?

☐ Will you find out what you want to learn if you ask these questions?

Now take your survey. Keep these points in mind:

Decide who your audience is, and ask people in that group.
Decide whether to take your survey by mail, by phone, or in person.
Ask enough people so that your results are a good sample of the
way people in your audience feel.

3. You might want to use the space below to create a graph that will help you understand
the information.

On a separate piece of paper, analyze your results.

30
LESSON

Contrasting Landscapes
Writing Descriptions

What You'll LEARN
You can apply your knowledge of earth science to contrasting two landscapes.

What You'll DO
These two photographs each contain different examples of the physical changes that can occur to the earth. Closely observe these photographs and identify the physical features in each. Then contrast—find the differences—in the features and the forces that formed each landscape.

What You'll WRITE

1. Use this chart to contrast the physical features of the two landscapes.

	Mountain photograph	**Shore photograph**
Major physical features		
Forces that shaped the landscape		

2. Using the chart you completed above, write a paragraph contrasting the two landscapes and the forces that created them. _____

_____

_____

_____

_____

_____

_____

_____

_____

_____

_____

_____

_____

_____

_____

31 Explaining Science
LESSON
Writing a Tip Sheet

What You'll LEARN

Often, when people have something they want many people to know about, they write a news release or a tip sheet to explain it. They send this tip sheet to newspaper, radio, and television reporters to let them know about an event or important news. You will learn how to write a tip sheet for science topics.

What You'll Do

People have become very interested in environmental and other science news. You can write a tip sheet based on one of the following events or on something you have been studying, such as:

a news conference to discuss the discovery of a new drug that helps heal broken bones

the announcement of a new recycling program

a news conference to discuss new information about global warming

A tip sheet follows the 5Ws of newspaper reporting: Who? What? When? Where? and Why? People who write tip sheets about science issues have to be careful to use language that people who are not scientists can understand. If they are explaining a new way of doing things, you need to write a step-by-step process.

Who: Who is making the announcement or is involved in the event? Give a description of this person or people.

What: What is the subject of the announcement or event?

When: When will the announcement be made, or when did the event happen?

Where: Where will the announcement be held, or where did the event take place?

Why: Why is this news conference, announcement, or event important? This section should include some background information and give the reporter a sense of why his or her audience would be interested in this information. Because this is a tip sheet about science, it is important to link the event or announcement to the reading audience's everyday life, if possible.

Here is one example:

Hobein University

12000 Campus Avenue • (303) 333-1000 • Fax: (303) 333-1010

Who: Dr. Martha Gray, professor of pediatrics, Hobein University, 222-2986

What: Press Conference announcing the discovery of a new treatment for childhood ear infections.

When: Thursday, March 13, at 2 P.M.

Where: University Press Room, Blackmun Building, Hobein University

Why: Ear infections are one of the most common problems among children. These infections can lead to discomfort and even to loss of hearing. Dr. Gray's 17 years of research in this field have led to a groundbreaking discovery that she will announce at the news conference. This discovery may lead to the end of most childhood ear infections.

What You'll WRITE

Fill in these blanks to create your own tip sheet about an event that will happen soon in your school or your community. Be sure to include all of the information that a reporter would need to create a news story about it. You will probably need another piece of paper to finish answering "Why."

1. Who: _____

_____

2. What: _____

_____

_____

3. When: _____

_____

4. Where: _____

_____

5. Why: _____

_____

32 Writing Persuasively A Flyer

What You'll LEARN

Science writing isn't just reports. People often write on science topics to persuade people.

What You'll DO

Imagine you own a bicycle messenger service. You compete with companies that use cars and vans. You need to find new customers. First, though, you have to convince them to hire you.

You want to create a flyer you will send to businesses. In your flyer, you will explain why people should hire your company. You have decided to focus on the fact that your company is more environmentally friendly than companies that use cars and vans. Research the facts about air pollution to help you write your flyer.

Usually, a flyer is a one-page piece of paper that tries to persuade someone to use the product or service written about in the flyer.

Here are some tips about writing to persuade:

1. Remember that what you write is intended to persuade the reader to do something. Think of how the reader will benefit.

2. When you are writing about science topics that people will not easily understand, use simple language. Explain the background behind the science.

3. Because you are writing about science, which people sometimes don't understand, be careful about writing facts. Make sure you are honest about the way you interpret facts.

4. List only several strong reasons instead of many less important reasons.

5. Make a strong concluding argument. Sum up your strongest point or points at the end of your argument.

Here are several layouts of flyers that are intended to persuade:

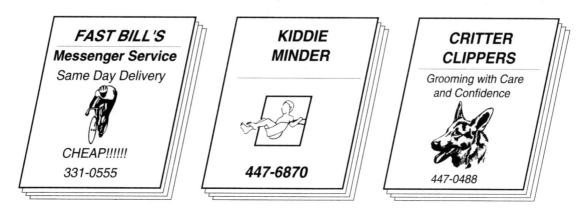

FAST BILL'S
Messenger Service
Same Day Delivery

CHEAP!!!!!!
331-0555

KIDDIE MINDER

447-6870

CRITTER CLIPPERS
Grooming with Care and Confidence

447-0488

What You'll WRITE Create the copy for your flyer. Remember, also, to include the information people will need: *Who, What, When, Where,* and *Why.*

_____

_____

_____

_____

_____

_____

_____

_____

_____

_____

_____

_____

_____

_____

_____

After you finish your work, ask a classmate to play the role of a homeowner who just picked up the flyer. On a separate piece of paper, write your classmate's answers to these questions:

Is this flyer persuasive? Why or why not? Give an example.
How would you improve this flyer?
What questions do you have after reading the flyer?

Science at Work

LESSON 33 Interpreting a Table
The Best Dog Food

What You'll LEARN

When you interpret data, or information, in a table, you explain its meaning. People are often called on to interpret information in tables. Two examples of this are railroad schedules and tables that compare miles per gallon in a review of cars.

What You'll DO

You work for a veterinarian. Lately she's been unhappy with the dog food she sells. She has put you in charge of finding a replacement food to sell to her clients. You bought four different kinds of food. Then you designed an experiment to find out which the dogs like best and which are best for the dogs. Here is the data you collected on the dog foods. Each dog was fed the correct amount for its size once daily. Each dog was fed each kind of food for a week.

BOXER	Food #1	Food #2	Food #3	Food #4
energy level	high	medium	high	low
appearance of coat	glossy	glossy	glossy	dull
amount dog ate	all	1/2	1/2	1/3
general health	excellent	excellent	good	good

SPANIEL	Food #1	Food #2	Food #3	Food #4
energy level	medium	low	high	medium
appearance of coat	flaking skin	glossy	glossy	medium
amount dog ate	2/3	all	all	all
general health	fair	fair	excellent	good

POODLE	Food #1	Food #2	Food #3	Food #4
energy level	high	high	high	medium
appearance of coat	glossy	glossy	glossy	glossy
amount dog ate	all	all	all	2/3
general health	excellent	excellent	excellent	good

TERRIER	Food #1	Food #2	Food #3	Food #4
energy level	medium	medium	high	high
appearance of coat	flaking skin	glossy	dull	glossy
amount dog ate	1/2	1/2	2/3	all
general health	fair	fair	fair	excellent

What You'll WRITE
Study all the data and interpret it. Create a graph that shows you the information visually. (To review how to make a graph, see Analyzing Information: Creating a Bar Graph, in Lesson 9, on page 18.) Then answer these questions.

1. What characteristics do the tables measure? Why are these important? _____

_____

_____

_____

2. Does one food seem clearly better than the others? Why? _____

_____

_____

_____

3. On another piece of paper, write your recommendation to the veterinarian. She can choose to carry one food. You could also recommend that she carry several brands. Be sure to give reasons for your choice.

34 Observing a Photograph
LESSON

Writing a Description

What You'll LEARN After carefully observing this photograph, you can identify and describe it.

What You'll DO You work for a publishing company. You've just been given the photograph below. It will be included in a book about nature. Your job is to write a caption for it. Unfortunately, the editor lost the information the photographer gave him. Use your powers of observation to notice the details and correctly describe the ecosystem (the kind of environment) in a caption.

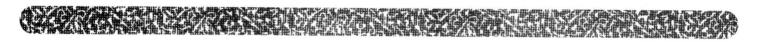

What You'll   Answer these questions as you observe the details—the shapes, sizes, shades,
WRITE   and textures—in the photograph on the previous page.

1. What can you tell about the amount of rain that falls here? Why do you think this?

_____

_____

_____

_____

_____

2. What can you tell about the ability of this habitat to support life? Why do you think this?

_____

_____

_____

_____

_____

3. What do you think these animals eat? Why? _____

_____

_____

_____

_____

4. What do you think these animals use for shelter? Why? _____

_____

_____

_____

5. Write the caption for the photograph here. Remember to use precise words.
Explain science terms in simple language. _____

_____

_____

_____

_____

_____

35 Explaining Science
Writing for Children

What You'll LEARN

One of the important skills in science is being able to explain what you know. On these pages, you'll explain the development of an idea in science in a picture book so that a first grader can understand it.

What You'll DO

First, choose a topic in the history of science that interests you. Here are some possibilities:

    the invention of electricity
    the discovery of the solar system
    the history of how a polio vaccine was created
    the history of nuclear energy

Research your topic. Take notes about what you discover. Then organize what you learned into a story that a first grader can understand. Write possible ways to illustrate each page.

What You'll WRITE

1. On the rest of this page, use a graphic organizer to plan the flow of ideas in your book.

2. Make a thumbnail sketch (a small version of the pages in your book) on this page. Write the words as they would appear. Also write what illustrations or drawings you would like to see. If you need more pages, use another piece of paper.

After you've finished your thumbnail sketch, make a full-sized book. Give it to a first grader to see if he or she understands your idea.

36 Explaining Science
Weathercasting

LESSON

What You'll LEARN   Weathercasters combine science and an entertaining style to please the people who watch them. They also have to present their explanation of the weather in a short period of time. Now you'll see if you can do as well.

What You'll Do   Study the weather map of the United States below.

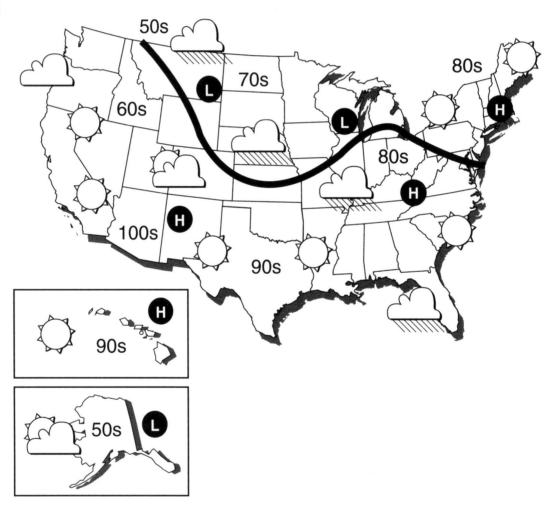

Do you understand the symbols on the map and what they mean? Answer these questions that explain the map, if you can. If you can't, do some research and then answer them.

What You'll WRITE

1. What does the *H* on the map mean? _____

_____

_____

2. What does the *L* mean? _____

_____

3. What does the large curved line mean? _____

_____

You have to write the 30-second national weather script for the weathercaster to read while this map is behind him. The map is for the next day's weather. Use this checklist as you write the script.

❑ Are you using simple words that are easy to say and understand?

❑ Is the tone conversational, as if you were talking to a friend?

❑ Have you explained why there will be a certain kind of weather tomorrow?

❑ Are all the important weather trends for the next day mentioned?

❑ Have you read the script to see if it is 30 seconds long?

4. Write your script here. _____

_____

_____

_____

_____

_____

_____

_____

_____

_____

_____

_____

_____

_____

_____

37 Explaining Science
Simple Machines

LESSON

What You'll LEARN
Learning to write about science is a useful skill. It can help you understand how machines work.

What You'll DO
Each of these drawings illustrates a simple machine. Create a matching test for a second-grade textbook. Describe how each machine works and tell which kind of machine it is. Then create the answer key for the test.

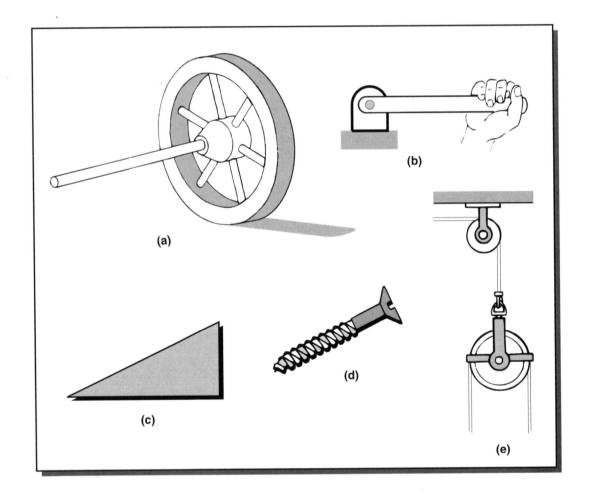

(a)

(b)

(c)

(d)

(e)

What You'll WRITE
Use another piece of paper to write your test. In language a second grader will understand, write what each machine is and describe what it does. Give two examples of each machine. A see-saw is an example of a lever, for example. Write the answer key at the bottom of the sheet.

Writing Checklist

You may write a letter to apply for a job or a letter to a friend about a baseball game. No matter what you're writing, you can use this checklist to help you make sure that your ideas are heard and understood.

Prewriting. Before you pick up a pencil, you need to do some thinking about what you'll write and how you'll write. Answer these questions as you plan your writing:

❏ What is my purpose? Why am I writing? What message do I want to communicate?

❏ Who is my audience? Who will read my work? Answering this question will help you decide how you will write. If you are writing a letter to apply for a job, your letter will probably be formal. If it is a letter to a friend, your letter will have a friendlier tone.

❏ What kind of writing will I be doing? There are many different types of writing. These include letters, speeches, notes, and reports. You need to decide which kind of writing you'll be doing.

Research and Organizing. You need to know what you're writing about. In research papers, you may be doing formal research. In letters to persuade, you may need to gather facts. In this stage, you need to find information about your subject.

❏ Should I write an outline? For most types of writing, it makes sense to outline or even make a brief list of your main points. When you write your first draft, you can turn your outline into paragraphs.

Drafting. This is where you write the information you've gathered. In this stage, don't worry about grammar or punctuation. Put your ideas down, keeping these questions in mind:

❏ Do I have an introduction that tells the reader what I plan to say?

❏ Do I make my main points and use details to support them?

❏ Does my writing flow from one point to the next?

❏ Does my conclusion briefly restate the main point of the writing?

Revising. Here are questions to think about as you look over and revise your first draft:

❏ Have I checked my spelling, grammar, and punctuation?

❏ Have I read my writing to see if I can use better words or cut out unnecessary ones?

❏ Is my writing interesting? Would other people want to read it?

Preparing a Final Copy. After you have revised your writing, share it with a friend. Ask him or her the questions in the drafting and revising sections. Use the responses as a guide to creating your final draft. Then write or type a clean copy of your work.